FANSHAWE COLLEGE

Published in 2007 by
Binea Press, Inc.
512-1673 Richmond Street
London, Ontario, Canada N6G 2N3

Tel: 519.660.6424
Fax: 519.660.4449

E-mail: bineapress@bellnet.ca
www.bineapress.com

Distributed by:

Binea Press Inc.
519.660.6424

Library and Archives Canada Cataloguing in Publication

Bain, Richard (Richard G.), 1954-

Fanshawe College / author / photographer, Richard Bain

Foreword by Anne Marie DeCicco-Best

Text by Hank Daniszewski

ISBN 978-0-9783012-3-1

1. Fanshawe College – Pictorial works. I. Daniszewski, Hank II. Title.

LE3.F35B34 2007   378.713'26   C2007-905963-5

Copyright © 2007 by Binea Press, Inc.

Design by Response Generators
London, Ontario, Canada
Tel: 519.432.4932
www.rgdirect.com

Printed in Canada by Friesens Corporation
Altona, Manitoba

FANSHAWE COLLEGE

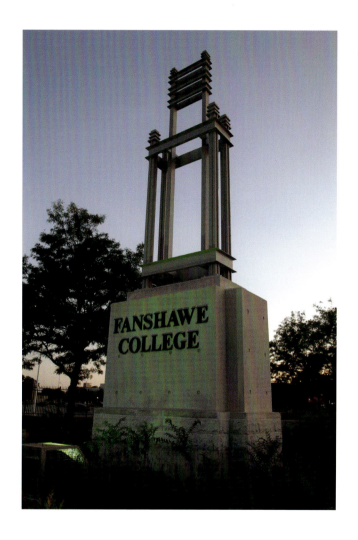

RICHARD BAIN

Foreword by
Anne Marie DeCicco-Best

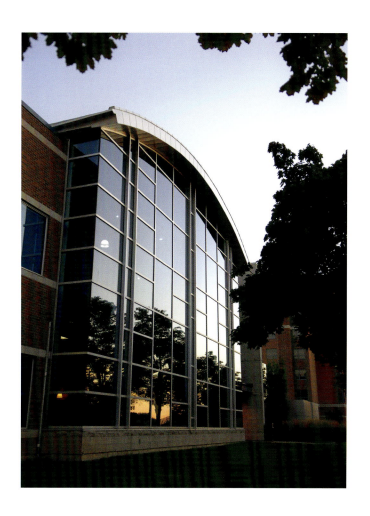

*With gratitude and affection,
this book is dedicated to*

Bob and Shelly Siskind

Foreword

Against the backdrop of Fanshawe College's 40th anniversary, I can't help calling to mind those first few days on campus when I was bursting with excitement and wonder.

I walked through the doors full of hope and anticipation, even a little nervous of what was to come. Two years later, I walked out, prepared to take on the world, ready to embrace new opportunities.

Although I held no political aspirations at the time, I knew I wanted to make a difference and I believed the College experience would help me find the best way to do it. As a student of the Broadcast Journalism program, the arduous training brought into focus a heightened awareness of the community I lived in and an understanding that every decision made played an important part in shaping London's future.

Even so, how could I have known those middle of the night production runs would provide me with the discipline and commitment to meet any challenge. Or that working on air, broadcasting news and researching stories, would prepare me, as Mayor, to address crowds of thousands or promote London as a great place to live, to create jobs, to attract investment and to live your dreams.

I was inspired to be more than I thought I could be, to reach new heights and discover the gifts that make me the person I am today. I have become a stronger person, a better journalist, and eventually, an effective ambassador for my community.

Enjoying the summer sun in M Building.

H Building, built in 1990.

From its humble beginnings in 1967 with just over seven hundred students on site, today's College now serves more than forty-five thousand students in expanding campuses across four different communities. Just walking through the corridors and from one building to another, one can witness progress in action: more state-of-the-art facilities, new exciting courses to match today's emerging trends, and a campus rich in diversity. Yet, the bricks and mortar only tell part of the story. For its students, Fanshawe continues to be a place to develop life skills, have fun, and create lasting friendships for the future. I know this to be true because some of my fellow students are still the closest friends and colleagues I have today.

Thanks to the solid foundation poured out through my Fanshawe College experience, it gave me the determination, work ethic and desire to build a career that changes people's lives and makes a positive difference. I'm privileged to be London's Mayor and I'm proud to be a Fanshawe grad. I'm grateful for all the hard work I was asked to do and all the friends I made along the way. Indeed, Fanshawe will always be about learning, yearning and living your dream and Richard Bain's amazing photos certainly encapsulate the College's energy and passion from days gone by, with a glimpse of what is yet to be.

Enjoy!

Mayor Anne Marie DeCicco-Best

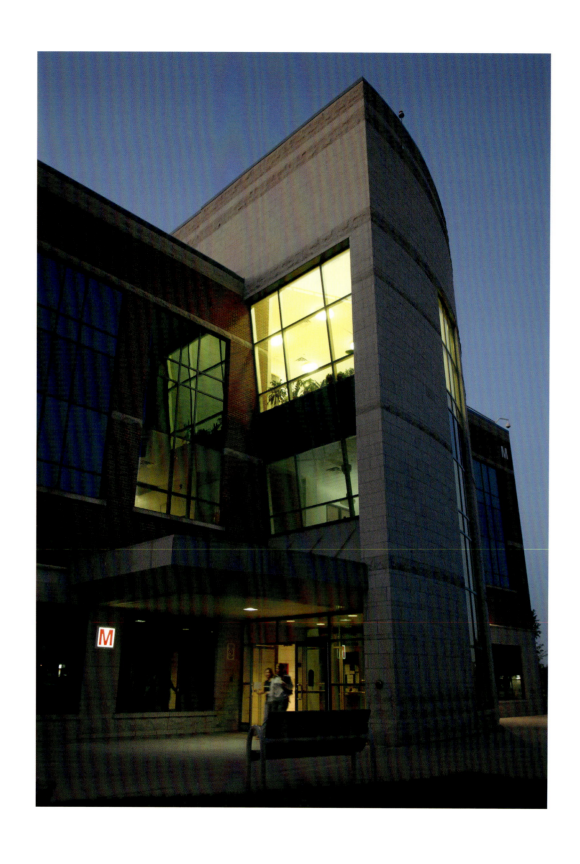

Students heading home after evening Continuing Education classes.

The Centre for Construction Trades and Technology
was built in phases and completed in 2006.

"It's a fabulous place. I said it all the years I worked there and I say it now, I was proud to be a part of its history."

Roberta Spence
One of the original 1967 staff who officially retired in 2001
but came back to work twice for extended periods.

Winter's artistry after an ice storm.

Business students in a workshop.

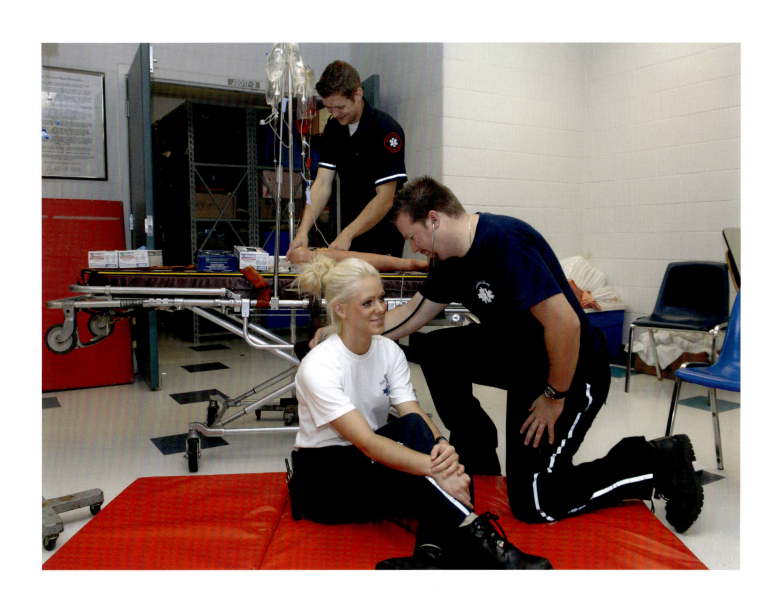

Students enrolled in the paramedic program practise
various scenarios, preparing themselves for a career helping others.

Nursing students take a break from clinical studies to rehearse the health promotion dance.

Fanshawe's First Nations Centre hosts their annual Year-End Social Gathering.

Taking a break from studies at the basketball court outside Peregrine House residence.

Enjoying pool in The Gamesroom in the Student Union Building.

"Community colleges are no longer a fallback choice to university. Many students coming out of high school are making Fanshawe their first choice because it offers the education they need for a specific career."

*Randy Dafoe
President of the Fanshawe Alumni Association*

THE SISKIND GALLERY IS USED BY MANY PROGRAMS TO SHOWCASE STUDENT WORK.

The Fashion Design program prepares students for careers in the world of fashion.

ONE OF THE MANY HOMEWORK AND LEARNING LABS ON CAMPUS.

The food court in the D E F Junction is a popular meeting place between classes.

above: Fanshawe's Student Centre showcases some magnificent architecture.

right: Reading outside B Building between classes.

Students moving into residence and some helpful directions during orientation.

This metal sculpture in the Centre for Construction Trades and Technology is one of the creations of the "Welding Wonders" project created by students in the Fine Art Program with materials donated by John Zubick Ltd.

Students work on year-end projects in the Fashion Merchandising program.

The "Sweet Escape", a wearable art fashion show where everything is made from candy, is a fundraiser for the London Humane Society.

top: Technology students at work.

above: Getting ready to ship a
prefabricated garden shed to a customer.

left: Building Technology students craft projects
on tables made from the old B gymnasium floor.

Heading to class through the new entrance to B Building.

"I've been a Fanshawe teacher for twenty years and it has never been boring. No two years have been exactly the same and I've been challenged and engaged by the work we do."

Kim Cechetto
English as a Second Language
Co-ordinator, Language and Liberal Studies

ENGLISH AS A SECOND LANGUAGE STUDENTS ENJOY A HANDS-ON LESSON ABOUT NEWFOUNDLAND.

A warm spring day on campus.

38

The Woodstock Campus, surrounded by beautiful gardens and a water park, can be enjoyed during this study session in the cafeteria.

President Howard Rundle and Mayor Anne Marie DeCicco-Best unveil the street sign celebrating the renaming of Second Street to Fanshawe College Boulevard to commemorate the College's 40th anniversary.

Artist Frances Gage celebrated with the College by rededicating her sculpture the "Discovery of Hands."

"Fanshawe's evolution has never been constant or rigid. It adapts and adapts. That's one of its greatest strengths."

*Fred Galloway
Fanshawe Board of Governors
Chair 2007-2008*

JANUARY ON THE LONDON CAMPUS OUTSIDE H AND M BUILDINGS.

Winter in Woodland Gardens at the London campus.

"Fanshawe is about dreams...
The dream of a fulfilling and challenging career,
the dream of a better life."

Howard Rundle
Fanshawe President

Fanshawe's Men's Soccer team scores during their home opener.

Ranked top in the province, Fanshawe's Women's Basketball team on the offensive.

"Businesses understand the tremendous economic engine they have in Fanshawe. They supply Fanshawe with whatever they manufacture from tractors to tools, so students can train on up-to-date equipment."

Bob Siskind
President of Decade Corporation, Chair Capital Campaign and Chair Fanshawe College Foundation.

AT WORK ON A PROJECT IN A WELDING LAB.

This classroom is integrated into the Truck Shop for hands-on learning.

Latin dancing is part of Salsa Caliente, a Fanshawe student celebration.

Kimonos designed and modeled by students at the Asian Occasion Gala.

top: Working outside in the D courtyard.

above: Planning a getaway in a Travel and Tourism lab.

54

The retail corridor outside of the College stores.

Early morning "Rush Hour" in front of the London Campus.

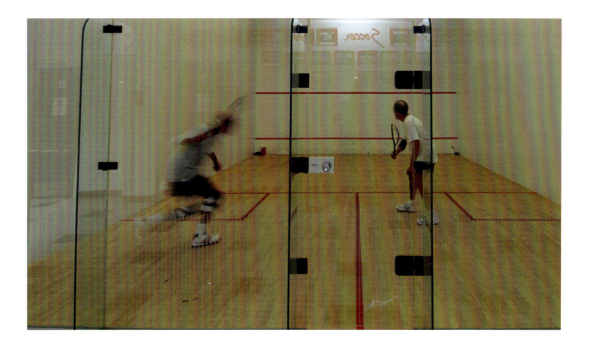

The London Campus has excellent on-site recreational facilities.

Art students create magnificent pieces in the Fine Art program.

58

Finished Fanshawe work is proudly displayed at Western's McIntosh Gallery.

ABOVE: THE STUDENT UNION EXECUTIVE AND MASCOT FREDDIE THE FALCON PREPARE TO HELP OUT DURING ORIENTATION.

RIGHT: FANSHAWE'S STUDENT UNION IS HOUSED IN THIS MAGNIFICENT BUILDING.

Fanshawe College boasts an impressive library. Information can be accessed both online and in person.

Fanshawe's Health Sciences area includes, among others, dental and nursing programs. Facilities are among the finest in the country.

TOP: Fanshawe Chorus London and The Gerald Fagan Singers rehearsing for one of many upcoming performances.

ABOVE: Staff from The James N. Allan Campus in Simcoe represent Fanshawe at the Norfolk County fair.

Theatre Arts students perform at the Galleria Campus.

above: The chef not only prepares,
but plates and serves during the Gala.

left: Finishing touches in the hospitality
program before the community Gala.

At work in the Culinary programs.

"The Fanshawe Student Union has always been innovative - always progressive. It has played a real leadership role for all community colleges."

Brad Forwell
Fanshawe Student Union President in 1980 when the first Student Union building, financed with student fees, was opened.

THIS HALLWAY BOASTS AN IMPRESSIVE STAINED GLASS CEILING, OUTSIDE THE OUTBACK SHACK.

Fanshawe's broadcast newsroom is one of the largest in the country.

"I feel to this day, after graduating and leaving the College in 1980, a very special connection to Fanshawe and to its students. I consider myself part of the Fanshawe family. If we see each other in the trenches somewhere, come and look me up and you'll have a friend in the field."

Dana Lewis
Broadcaster, FOX News Channel (FNC) based in Moscow

CIXX-FM, known as "The X", was Canada's first fully-licensed student radio station.

A setting sun through the pergola in Woodland Gardens.

"Discovery of Hands" graces the outside of F Building.

Evening at the St. Thomas/Elgin Campus.

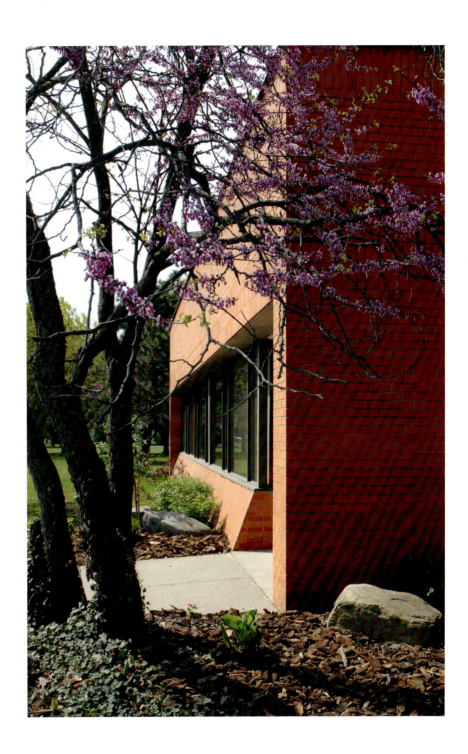

The James N. Allan Campus in Simcoe.

Students working at the Spriet Family Greenhouse as part of their program.

ABOVE: HORTICULTURE STUDENTS CREATE
NEW GARDENS IN FRONT OF THE GATES.

LEFT: THE NEW GATES ALONG FANSHAWE COLLEGE BOULEVARD.

85

CTV News President Robert Hurst addresses journalism and television students in the Broadcast Centre.

Learning to take "product" photographs in the studio.

"The Fanshawe journey has been incredible; working here, graduating from here, having my children go here, and making lifelong friendships has been amazing."

*Dorothy Gryszczuk
Co-op Officer, Fanshawe College*

ABOVE: END OF SEMESTER EXAMS IN J GYM.

LEFT: HEADING HOME AT THE END OF THE DAY.

Laying down another track in the MIA recording studio.

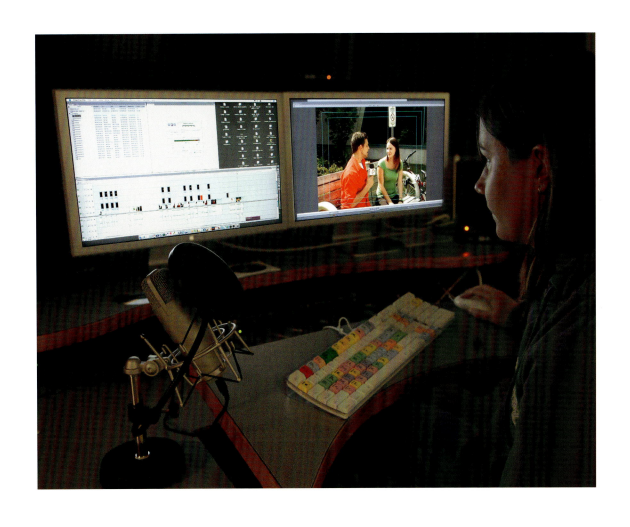

above: Working in the edit studio.

left: Ready to go "On Air" in Studio One at FCTV.

"We are going to be totally dependent on our intellect, on our ability to compete in the world community and you can only do this through a superior education system."

Bill Davis
Founder of Ontario's community college system
speaking to graduates at Fanshawe's 40th graduation ceremonies.

Hitting the books in Falcon House.

*"We really prided ourselves on booking up-and-coming acts...
We pushed the envelope of entertainment."*

*John b. Young
Fanshawe Student Union Operations Manager,
former Student Council President and SUB's entertainment programmer*

RIGHT: THE STUDENT CENTRE.

ABOVE: ENJOYING FRIENDSHIPS IN THE OUTBACK.

Winter reflections at the London Campus.

top: Carrying the tools of her trade across campus.

above: students working on their assignments.

right: The morning winter sun, reflected off the windows in M Building.

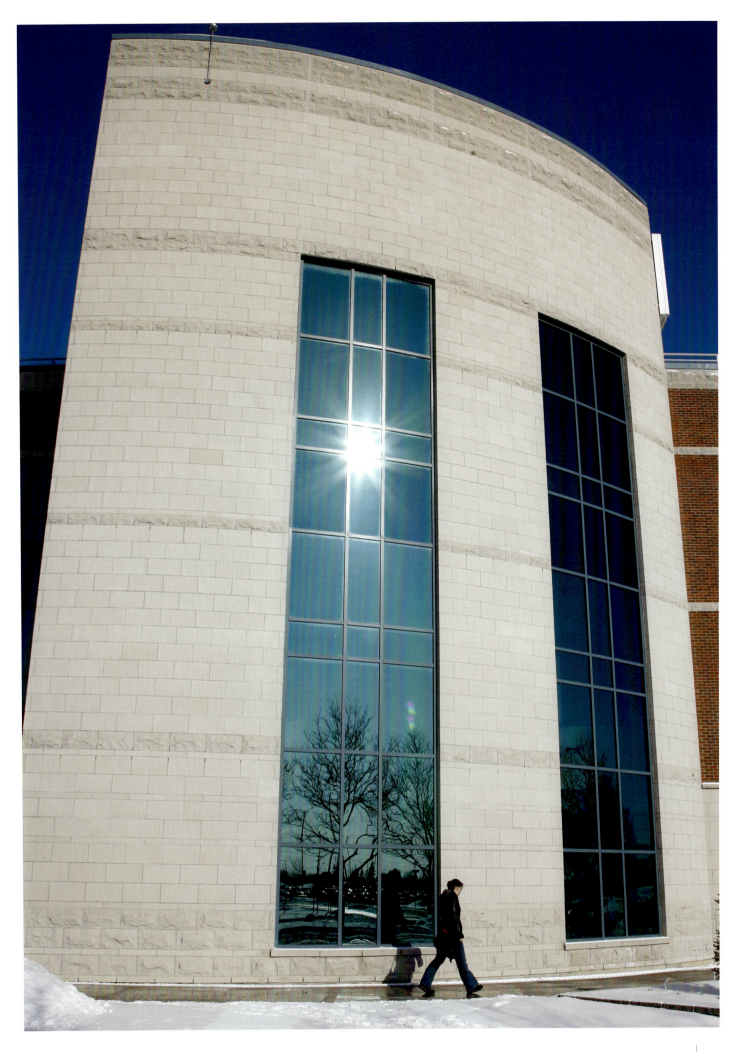

An Early Childhood Education student enjoys time at her placement at Bonaventure Meadows Children's Centre.

Students from Recreation and Leisure Services preform a team-building initiative.

103

The walkway through D Building.

Autumn on campus.

TOP: WATCHING THE PROCESSION AT GRADUATION.

ABOVE: THE HONOURABLE WILLIAM DAVIS, FORMER PREMIER OF ONTARIO, SHARES SOME MEMORIES WITH PRESIDENT HOWARD RUNDLE.

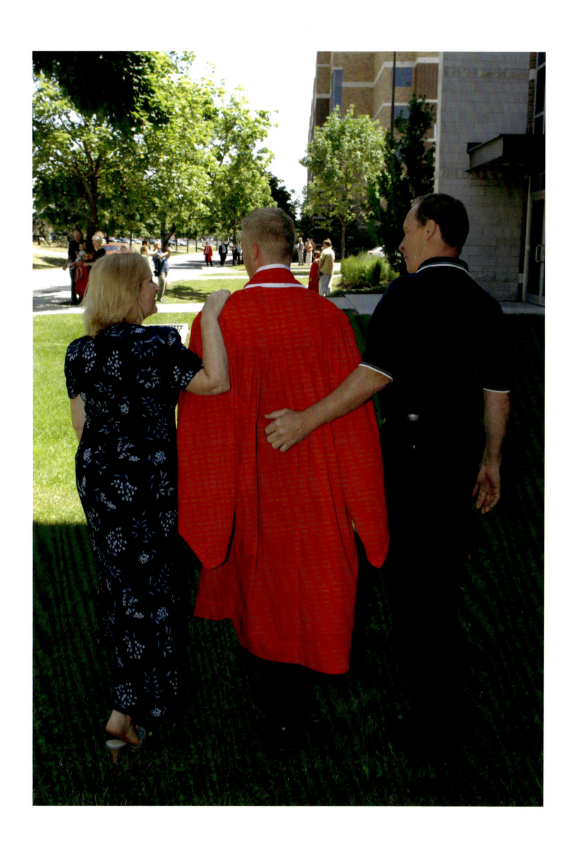

Proud parents spend time with their new grad.

Heading off to the "real world" with thousands of memories and promising careers.

"The teachers accommodated your needs and personalized your program whether you were a single mom or an athlete like myself. They made it easy to socialize and connect with a great group of friends."

Danielle Campo
Fanshawe's 100,000th graduate
and Pan-American swimming champion

ENJOYING THE MOMENT AFTER GRADUATION.

History of Fanshawe College

By Hank Daniszewski

Like most successful inventions, Fanshawe College was born out of necessity and has evolved with the times.

It was 1967, Canada's centennial year. In a decade marked by remarkable growth and change, Fanshawe was one of nineteen community colleges established by the Ontario government in a bold experiment to create an entirely new branch of education.

Canada was riding an unprecedented wave of confidence, optimism and unity with millions flocking to Expo 67 in Montreal. The Beatles had released the Sgt. Pepper's album; hippies were celebrating the summer of love and the Toronto Maple Leafs were still a winning team, taking the Stanley Cup.

It was a different era, as Fanshawe College President Howard Rundle noted in a graduation address forty years later. "Canada must have looked very bright indeed that year. Our society was so upbeat and confident that 720 people could enrol in an institution they knew nothing about to take programs they could not possibly be sure would lead to employment and a better life." Perhaps the confidence was born of the realization that community colleges like Fanshawe could solve two urgent needs in the province – a huge wave of baby boomers flooding through the education system and a surging economy that created jobs requiring technical skills.

John Robarts, a Londoner and former Education Minister, was Premier of Ontario and Bill Davis was the new Education Minister. Both men were struggling to guide Ontario through spectacular growth in the education system caused by the surge of births which began after the Second World War and peaked in 1960.

JOHN ROBARTS (RIGHT), PREMIER OF ONTARIO (1961-1971), AT THE OPENING OF THE OVC.

The Ministry of Education had created new vocational and technical high schools as well as a new four-year program to recognize the needs of students who were headed for the workforce. But what caught Queen's Park off guard was that these boomers were not dropping out of high school like their parents. In 1946 about sixty-three percent of students dropped out of high school. By 1964 the dropout rate had fallen to twenty-six percent. Meanwhile the Ontario economy was thriving, buoyed by the signing of the Auto Pact in 1965, which reinforced the province's manufacturing sector. New technologies in offices and hospitals were creating jobs that had never existed before and employers were in urgent need of workers who could hit the ground running.

Against this backdrop, Davis made a landmark speech to the Ontario Legislature on May 21, 1965, proposing the creation of a community college system. In his speech Davis recognized that the "knowledge explosion" had created a new economy in the province that would require almost all high school graduates to get some form of postsecondary education. There had been concerns that new technology would displace workers and drive up unemployment. Instead it had created an urgent need for graduates with new skills. "No employer would dare or could afford to entrust some of the new complex and expensive machines to the inept handling of an unskilled, poorly-educated employee," said Davis.

But where would these people come from? Davis noted that Ontario's universities had neither the space nor the type of programs to turn out the graduates that were needed.

"It is not feasible, nor indeed desirable that all graduates of high school should go to university. The real need of a substantial number of our young people lies elsewhere. They would be served poorly and fare poorly in our traditional university system."

Before setting up the system, Davis toured community college systems in California and Florida. He decided against an American-style junior college system where technical training was combined with academic credits that could be transferred to a university after a year or two of study. Davis reasoned the junior colleges were not an appropriate fit for Ontario's high school system, which had both a five-year system for university preparation, and a four-year system focused on vocational education. Instead Ontario's community colleges would concentrate on technical education, both full- and part-time, suited to the needs of the job market and adult education in the community.

The colleges were to be entirely separate from universities and would grant diplomas rather than degrees. In contrast, British Columbia and Alberta were planning community college systems much closer to the American junior college model. In the view of future Fanshawe President Harry Rawson, the blueprint Davis laid out was "enlightened" and created a unique system for Ontario. "It made the community colleges different from universities – a true alternative rather than a watered-down version."

Davis also decided that to keep costs down and keep the community focus, the new Ontario system would be based on "commuter colleges" that would not provide student residences. The community colleges would each serve one of nineteen distinct geographic areas established by the province. Area 11, including the City of London, and the counties of Middlesex, Elgin, Oxford, and Norfolk would become the future home of Fanshawe. The restrictions on residences and co-operation with universities were seen by some as a mistake but it would take many years before those barriers started to crumble.

A Council of Regents was created to supervise the provincial system, but each college would have its own Board of Governors with some degree of local autonomy.

The community college system had to be created in a hurry to meet the urgent need. Centennial College in Scarborough opened barely a year after Davis first proposed the system in the Legislature. Fortunately, the system did not have to start entirely from scratch. Ryerson had opened in 1948 in Toronto as Ontario's first Institute of Technology and similar schools in Hamilton, Ottawa and Windsor were added later.

In 1963, as a first tentative step toward meeting the need for technical education, the provincial government created new Ontario Vocational Centres, including one in London. Rawson, a London native and technical teacher at H.B. Beal Secondary Commercial and Technical High School was chosen as the first principal of the London OVC. The provincial government selected a fifteen-acre site on Oxford Street east of Highbury Avenue for the London OVC. The site was once part of a two hundred-acre farm attached to the London Asylum, later to become the London Psychiatric Hospital.

The Ontario Vocational Centre London (OVCL) opened in September 1964 with a staff of thirty and three hundred students. Initially there were only some portable classrooms and the two buildings which later became the core of Fanshawe's B and C buildings. The OVCL offered a mixture of trades courses including electronics, welding and drafting as well as business and secretarial courses.

Rawson faced a challenge in hiring staff right from the beginning because the province was facing a serious teacher shortage at the time. Teachers' colleges were turning out only about ten percent of the graduates needed to serve Ontario's soaring enrolment.

THE PORTABLES, BUILT IN 1966.

Soon after Ontario Vocational Centres were set up, it became obvious they would not be enough to meet the demand for technical education. With Davis' speech in the Legislature, plans were set in motion to make the London OVC the foundation of a new community college.

The first meeting of the Fanshawe Board of Governors was held on September 13, 1966. John G. Laurie, an executive at 3M Canada was selected as the first Chairperson. R.M. Dillon, Dean of the Faculty of Engineering at The University of Western Ontario, served as Vice-Chairperson and Dr. Douglas Bocking, Dean of the Faculty of Medicine, was also on the Board.

One of the first issues was selecting a name for the new College. The governors invited the public to submit names for the new institution. Some of the suggestions included Tecumseh, Malahide, Central Erie, Governor Simcoe and E.V. Buchanan. In October, following community consultation, the Board selected Fanshawe, an old English word meaning "temple in the woods." Fanshawe was already the name of a nearby dam, lake and conservation area, but the name itself goes back to a small pioneer hamlet that was located at the corner of what is now Highbury Avenue and Fanshawe Park Road.

In December, the Board selected James A. Colvin as the first President of the new College. A native of Thunder Bay, Colvin served as a fighter pilot in the Second World War. After graduating from the University of Toronto and earning a doctorate in History and Politics at the University of London, he entered the diplomatic service. He served in the Department of External Affairs and was a senior official in the office handling relations with the United States.

Colvin was a firm believer in the social role of the new community colleges, proclaiming in an interview that they were the "biggest thing to hit education in this century." He set about putting his own stamp on Fanshawe. The College's original mandate was broadened to include more arts and social science-based programs with courses geared to jobs in areas such as child care and municipal government. Colvin saw Fanshawe as providing broad-based education and training to all ages and interest groups in the community. "There are virtually no limits to what it can do," he said in the original Fanshawe student handbook.

The Fanshawe Board of Governors approved an initial budget of $2.5 million. The school colours of red and white were chosen and the entire staff of the Ontario Vocational College was transferred over to Fanshawe.

But staying on the OVCL site on Oxford Street East was not a foregone conclusion. Even then, local politicians were talking about building a ring road around London, which had a population of about 200,000 at that time. A proposed cloverleaf would have been located just north of the new Fanshawe College campus. The Board of Governors considered other sites for expansion such as Wellington Road and Commissioners Road where the former Westminster Hospital was located.

On the first day of classes, September 1, 1967, registration was a casual affair. The students all showed up in the gym and lined up behind various banners marking their programs before heading off to their first class. Full-time students paid a $150 tuition fee and a $25 student activity fee.

Roberta Spence was one of the original Fanshawe employees, starting with OVCL and then moving into payroll and Fanshawe's Finance and Administration office. In the pre-computer age, Spence said there were only guidelines from the Ministry of Education. The administrative staff had to be creative and invent new systems to make the College function properly. "It was a close-knit group. We were pioneers and it was an adventure," said Spence.

Fanshawe's inaugural convocation was held on September 12, 1967 in Centennial Hall. Future Prime Minister Jean Chrétien, then a young junior cabinet minister, was a guest speaker.

B Building expansion.

Before the College even opened, the Board of Governors had held meetings in Oxford, Elgin and Norfolk to get public input on course offerings. Rawson became Fanshawe's Dean of Technology. It was an exciting time to be a teacher, he said, because they had the unprecedented freedom to create new courses. In the first few years enrolment and program offerings expanded rapidly to meet the needs of the community. But the rapid expansion put a physical and financial strain on the new campus. "We could never get anything in balance. If we had the staff we didn't have the textbooks; if we had the textbooks, we didn't have the space," said Rawson.

In August 1968 the Board of Governors expanded the original fifteen-acre campus site by acquiring another seventy-eight acres from the Ministry of Education. The property now stretched all the way back to Cheapside Street and no one at the time imagined that Fanshawe would ever run out of land. From then on the campus began its historic pattern of growing in a domino-like fashion with new buildings and additions added every few years to accommodate the growing enrolment and new programs and services.

In April of 1968 the Board approved the building of the East Annex later to be known as A building. The building was scheduled to open in September that year as a "temporary" structure. By December a second storey for the building was approved and the structure was completed about two years later. Before that project was even complete, the Board laid plans for a new structure to be known as D building that would provide a vital link between A, B and C. That building was completed in 1972 when enrolment had climbed to 3,300 full-time students. Even with all the construction, Fanshawe was required to rent space in a number of locations including two buildings on First Street, which housed the Design program and the Finance and Administration office.

In 1969 the Board of Governors approved a master plan for the future construction of the campus. But the plan was never really followed because it was overtaken by events and the uncertainties of government funding. Colvin said the lack of government funding put restraints on the growth of the College, forcing Fanshawe to turn away hundreds of applicants. Spence said budgeting was often a challenge for staff as well. "The Colleges could do so much more if we had more funding. But we had to work with what we had."

One example was the construction of A building, which came back to haunt the College. The campus library was moved from B building to the second floor of A. Support beams were installed on the first floor to support the weight of the books until a more permanent structure could be found. But as the years passed, the weight of the books provoked fears the second floor would collapse. The problem was finally resolved with the opening of the new Learning Resource Centre in 1982.

Fanshawe Presidents:
Dr. James A Colvin (1967 to 1979), Dr. Barry Moore (1987 to 1996),
Mr. Harry Rawson (1979 to 1987), Dr. Howard W. Rundle (1996 to present).

*"The community college is a major sociological breakthrough – an unconditional offer
of tertiary education. There are virtually no limits to what it can do, the courses
it can offer or the participation of its community."
(published in the 1967 student handbook)*

*J. A. Colvin
Fanshawe's first President*

The building boom and enrolment growth was constantly fueled by the new responsibilities being taken on by the community colleges in the 1970s. Community colleges became the obvious solution to many educational and training problems. From the beginning community colleges offered night school and extension courses aimed at the general public. In 1970 the colleges began to take responsibility for the job retraining programs sponsored by the federal government. Fanshawe also stepped in to help waves of new immigrants and foreign students with English as a Second Language programs.

To meet the needs for skilled labour in the community, a new program could be crafted around any area where there were jobs and student interest. Since government funding was based on per-student grants, a new course with good enrolment could be financially justified. Each division was backed by an industry advisory council that kept the College administration up-to-date on new job opportunities and changes in technology, especially important with the rapid evolution in computers and manufacturing equipment.

In 1970 Fanshawe started its first co-op program in Civil Engineering Technology. The co-op programs became a foundation of the College's close liaison with business and industry. Over the next eight years over thirty Fanshawe programs had a co-op component, more than any other college in Canada.

In the early years Fanshawe was already working with local hospitals in areas such as medical technology. In 1973 Fanshawe moved into training nurses, taking on administration of programs that had been delivered by the hospitals in London, Woodstock and St. Thomas.

In crafting programs, the staff also relied on the instincts and research of students enrolling in programs where they had identified job opportunities. A few programs went by the wayside, but the vast majority succeeded.

Some programs just seemed to grow spontaneously, such as the Music Industry Arts (MIA) program, which was launched in 1973 as Creative Electronics. The program started in an area known as the "fish bowl" because it was the site of a large aquarium associated with a Marine Biology program. Originally disguised as an option in the Fine Arts program to circumvent a bureaucratic approval process, the MIA program blossomed as students built their own recording studios and experimented with moog synthesizers. Tom Lodge, founder of the famous Radio Caroline private radio station in England, headed the program. Jack Richardson, a famed producer of acts such as the Guess Who, Pink Floyd and Peter Gabriel, joined the program's advisory board and later became a teacher. The new program provided a steady stream of producers, managers, technicians and performers for the Canadian music industry, which was thriving due to new requirements on broadcasters for Canadian content.

Fanshawe also broke into new areas such as the Radio and Television Arts program which eventually led to the creation of CIXX-FM – Canada's only CRTC licensed, course-run campus radio station. The station went on air in 1978 to serve the London market.

Fanshawe's Culinary Arts and Hospitality programs also led to the establishment of The Heliotrope, a fine-dining restaurant located on the campus, subsequently relocated and expanded to become Saffron's.

In 1977, the College grew again with the completion of E building. By that time the full-time enrolment had grown to 9,120.

After nearly 12 years in office, Colvin was succeeded by Harry Rawson. Rawson was selected over some high-profile figures who were rumored to be interested in the job, including former London Mayor Jane Bigelow and former provincial NDP leader Stephen Lewis. With his quiet manner and long experience that stretched back before the origins of Fanshawe, Rawson was seen as a President who could steer the College back into calmer waters. Enrolment and programs continued to expand with the opening of G building in 1984.

Rawson saw labour relations as one of the biggest challenges in the job. Shortly before he took office the College was embroiled in its first strike – a thirteen-day walkout by community college support workers across the province. The colleges' support staff and faculty had originally been represented by a provincial association. But in 1977 the Ontario Public Service Employees Union took over representation with separate locals for faculty and support staff. The first province-wide faculty strike took place in 1984, the first of three faculty strikes in Fanshawe's history. Rawson saw the province-wide structure for contract negotiations as a major obstacle to labour peace. "If the College could have negotiated directly with staff, a lot of this turmoil could have been avoided," he said.

Rawson had a cordial relationship with the Fanshawe Student Union (FSU). He is credited with crafting the deal that allowed the FSU to construct its own building on campus in 1980. "We always had the good fortune to have good, bright student Presidents. They were part of the solution, not the problem," said Rawson.

In 1987, Rawson retired as President and Barry Moore was hired as his successor. Moore came into the job with extensive experience, having served as President of two community colleges in British Columbia - Fraser Valley College in Chilliwack and Northern Lights in Dawson. A native of Toronto, Moore holds undergraduate degrees in Commerce and Divinity, a Masters of Sacred Theology and a Ph. D. in Educational Administration. He served as a United Church minister in northern Alberta and as University Chaplain at the University of Alberta. He entered the community college system by becoming the founding Chairperson of the Board of Grant MacEwan College in Edmonton.

Moore believed in the social role played by community colleges and saw them as an extension of his original career in the ministry. "I see it as a way of doing theology, enabling more life chances for people, many of whom were kicked around in life. People should have the capability to have a chance to fulfill their lives through education."

Moore's term saw more physical growth in the campus with the opening in 1990 of K building which housed the Child Care program and H building for the Nursing Assistant and Design programs. But he also faced a number of financial challenges. The faculty at Fanshawe participated in another province-wide strike in 1989 and soon after the province plunged into a recession in the 1990s. The provincial government forced a number of program cutbacks and made it difficult to launch any new initiatives. But enrolment continued to grow.

Moore focused on making Fanshawe a more integral part of the London community. In 1991 Fanshawe launched its first community fund-raising drive, something that was not allowed under the original community college mandate. Moore enlisted the help of Don Smith, co-founder of Ellis-Don, a London company that had grown to become a global leader in major construction projects such as Toronto's Skydome. Always a major supporter of Fanshawe, Smith had hired many graduates of the colleges and worked his community connections to make the fund-raising campaign a major success.

WORKING ON A METAL LATHE IN THE LATE SIXTIES.

Moore also worked to break down barriers with The University of Western Ontario by proposing better co-operation and the relaxation of rules that prevented the transfer of credits.

Moore retired in 1996 and was replaced by Howard Rundle. Like Rawson, Rundle had extensive experience at Fanshawe dating back to 1972 when he was hired as Director of Planning and Development. A native of Bowmanville, Rundle received his Ph.D. in Chemistry from the University of Toronto and served on the faculty of the University of Pittsburgh and York University. Rundle said he was frustrated by the emphasis on abstract research in the university environment. It was the opportunity to teach and be involved in more practical education that lured him from the university environment to Ontario's new community colleges. "All the research I did for my Master's and Ph.D., I can't imagine it did any good for anybody. I loved teaching and it was clear colleges placed a higher priority on it," said Rundle.

In 1999 Fanshawe marked another milestone with the construction of the first student residence. The $15 million building held four hundred students in comfortable quad-style living arrangements and gave the campus a new atmosphere that comes with full-time residents.

In 2000 the College embarked on a massive five-year $77 million building program in expectation of another enrolment surge as the children of baby boomers entered the postsecondary system.

In 2002 the number of first-year students at Fanshawe surpassed Western for the first time. The two institutions also made substantial progress in breaking down the old bureaucratic barriers with agreements to offer joint degree/diploma programs in areas such as Media, Communications, and Electronics. Colleges were also granted permission to offer applied degree programs, and Fanshawe announced two: Integrated Land Planning Technology and Bachelor of Applied Technology – Biotechnology.

The same year saw the opening of M building, which housed Communications and Design programs and the greenhouse complex known as N building. In 2003 a three-storey addition to F building was completed along with a second residence for four hundred students. The following year a new Student Centre, again owned and funded by the Student Union, was built between the two residences.

In 2005 the College went back to its roots with construction of a new $14 million Centre for Construction Trades and Technology. The new facility, known as T building, revamped the technical facilities that had once been the core of the College and allowed Fanshawe to address the shortage of trades and technology graduates.

As part of the overall construction boom, the Fanshawe campus was reoriented toward the east with a gateway leading to a courtyard area. It gave Fanshawe the "front door" that it had long lacked.

By now the growth of Fanshawe had reached a point that would have been considered unimaginable in 1967. The seventeen buildings on the London campus along with some much-needed green space now occupied almost the entire hundred-acre site. In 2006 the college purchased the former Small Business Centre a short distance from the campus, with an eye to further expansion of industrial and trades programs.

In 2007, Fanshawe launched its fortieth anniversary year with a number of community celebrations. London Mayor and Fanshawe graduate Anne Marie DeCicco-Best proclaimed that a portion of Second Street in front of the new entrance would be renamed Fanshawe College Boulevard.

Fanshawe is now the fifth largest community college in Ontario, with 120 program offerings and about fifteen thousand full-time students. In 2006, Danielle Campo, a student who overcame muscular dystrophy to win seven medals at the Paralympic Games, became Fanshawe's 100,000th graduate.

Fred Galloway, Chair of the Board of Governors for 2007-2008, says the College has thrived through constant change and has become a vital institution in London and southwestern Ontario. "Today Fanshawe is a leader in applied education and producing the graduates who drive virtually every dimension of community life," said Galloway.

Area Campuses

From its first days Fanshawe has functioned as a regional institution, and representatives from Oxford, Elgin and Norfolk counties have served on the Board of Governors.

Shortly after Fanshawe opened its doors, Woodstock became the site of the first area campus program in Farm Business Management providing basic agriculture and financial education to farm families close to home.

A similar program more closely geared to the needs of the tobacco belt was set up in Simcoe a year later. The first classes there were held on the second floor of a department store building and later moved to a former factory.

In 1969 Fanshawe College bought a former seniors' home from Oxford County for the bargain price of $7,500 as a new home for the Woodstock farm program. The 1893 building had served for many years as a House of Refuge for the destitute and mentally ill and was definitely a "fixer-upper." The basement had cells which had been used to detain intoxicated people and the second floor was in such rough shape it was blocked off on orders from the Fire Marshall.

In 1970, Fanshawe became a permanent presence in Elgin County when the community colleges took over employment retraining programs from the Board of Education. As a result, a centre on Ontario Road in St. Thomas was taken over by Fanshawe. Many of the programs offered at the St. Thomas campus were industrial and trades-related, reflecting the industrial base of the city.

The Woodstock and Simcoe campuses also grew by adding a broader base of programs geared to the wider community in areas such as business, trades and health care.

Part of the College's original mandate included extension courses and programs offered by the Community Services division. Over the years Fanshawe offered a variety of technical, vocational and general interest courses to the general public – everything from auto mechanics to belly dancing.

By 1968, Fanshawe was offering courses in Aylmer, Delhi, Ingersoll, Port Dover, Simcoe, St. Thomas, Strathroy, Tillsonburg, West Lorne and Woodstock. Through these retraining and extension programs, new immigrants learned to speak English, displaced workers learned new skills and many people pursued their hobbies and interests.

As far back as 1970 Fanshawe planned to have substantial area campuses in its region.

In 1979 the Simcoe campus moved into a new building. The new campus was named after James N. Allan, a local MPP, former provincial Treasurer and a strong supporter of Fanshawe.

In 1988 Fanshawe partnered with the City of Woodstock which was building a new multi-purpose facility to be known as the Woodstock District Community Complex. After almost 20 years in the old

Woodstock Campus in 1969.

"House of Refuge" Fanshawe opened a new and much larger campus in the landscaped complex which included a day care centre, double arena and community hall.

Fanshawe partnered with the Elgin County Roman Catholic Separate School Board, which was building a new high school in St. Thomas. After seven years of planning, the new $5.2 million campus was constructed adjacent to St. Joseph's High School. After many years on Ontario Road the St. Thomas campus moved to the new site in January 1997. Fanshawe and St. Joseph's share a gymnasium, a resource centre and cafeteria facilities in what was hailed as a model of community co-operation. Fanshawe's St. Thomas campus was expanded in 2001.

In 2004 Fanshawe made a substantial contribution to the resurgence of downtown London by leasing thirteen hundred square metres on the first floor of Galleria London's south wing to house the school's growing Theatre Arts program, Continuing Education classes and an employment service called Job Connect.

Student Life

When Ontario's community colleges first opened there was no model for student life outside the classroom, it had to be invented.

In the early days Fanshawe borrowed conventions from both high schools and universities. The Red and White Society ran the school dances and other social events. There was a cheerleading squad as well as various clubs and intramural sports. The first Student Council (later to evolve into the Fanshawe Student Union or FSU) was elected in 1967 with Bob Clark as President. Because the Council had no office, meetings were held under stairwells or in empty classrooms. Staff of the student newspaper Fanfare (later renamed the Fanshawe Dam and then the Interrobang) put the paper together on the stage in the gymnasium.

With Fanshawe located a good distance from the downtown pubs and bars, the FSU had an opportunity to develop a distinct social life on the campus. In the 1970s a new tradition was born with the Hiandrye, a student pub which operated on Thursdays and Fridays in the main cafeteria with live entertainment. Rock legend Bachman-Turner Overdrive was one of the bands playing the pubs in the early days. Major concerts were held at Wonderland Gardens several times a year and would sell more than one thousand tickets, representing over a quarter of the entire Fanshawe enrolment at the time.

The Student Union also operated a co-op store selling jeans, T-shirts and records. But with almost no continuity on the executive from year to year, the FSU was often disorganized with debt

AN EARLY NURSING GRADUATION – THE COLLEGE'S FIRST LOGO IS DISPLAYED.

accumulating from one year to the next. "We didn't know how to run our finances, we were often six months behind in the books and the new Council would find itself $30,000 in debt," said John b. Young, the Student Union President in 1975-76. The college administration sometimes had to advance funds to the Student Union to keep it from going bankrupt.

The situation reached a crisis point in 1976 when the election for Student Union President was declared invalid when it was discovered the winning candidate was no longer a student. The mismanagement in the FSU prompted the College's Student Services department to call for a partial takeover by the administration. A new election was held in the fall and Jim Young was elected president.

The same year Ralph Aston was hired as FSU's first full-time manager. Aston's hiring put the Student Union on a much firmer footing and allowed it to take on a more ambitious project, the building of the Student Union Building (SUB). It was a first for any community college in the province. The building was to be financed over a number of years by an annual $15 fee that students had approved in a referendum. The College's Board of Governors decided to extend the Student Union the $1.5 million needed for construction.

The SUB was completed in 1981 and included a large multi-purpose room for pubs, a variety store, as well as offices for the Student Union and the Interrobang. Brad Forwell, the Student Union President in 1980-81 said it was a milestone for student life on the campus. (Years later part of the building would be renamed as Forwell Hall). "It was a place to hang out and relax and not be watched by the school." Forwell said the FSU forged ahead taking a leadership role among community colleges in the province.

John b. Young, the former President, was hired as the SUB's building manager and entertainment programmer. With his experience as a rock music manager, he established the "nooner" – free noon concerts on Thursdays – which attracted a wide variety

117

of musicians and entertainers. One of the first bookings was a young comic impressionist named Jim Carrey who went on to become a Hollywood superstar. Other acts included the Bare Naked Ladies, Blue Rodeo, the Tragically Hip and Honeymoon Suite, a group that included two Fanshawe graduates.

With a small entertainment budget, Young said Fanshawe had to be innovative. "We really prided ourselves on up-and-coming acts that two years down the road would be the biggest things in the music industry." The Student Union also "pushed the envelope" over the years bringing in diverse acts such as female mud wrestlers, soap stars from The Young and the Restless, mentalist Mike Mandel and sex therapist Sue Johanson.

The students paid off the loan for the SUB ahead of schedule and a $2 million addition was added in 1995 including a new full-time bar and restaurant with a stained glass ceiling in the entrance.

Students continued to assert their rights both at the local and provincial level in areas such as tuition fees and classroom funding. In 1982 a thirty-hour sit-in was held by Advertising Arts students at the Applied Arts faculty office to protest outdated equipment and crowded classrooms. In 1986 Ontario students reached a milestone, gaining the right to have representation on college Boards of Governors.

In 1999 the character of the campus changed dramatically when Fanshawe's first student residence was constructed, followed by another in 2003.

In 2004 a new Student Union Building was opened between the two residences. The new Student Centre houses the Oasis dining centre, a health clinic and pharmacy as well as new offices for the Student Union and Interrobang.

The FSU also served older students who had young families. An annual Halloween party has always been a major draw as well as a PD-day program that allowed students to bring their children to school. In recent years the social needs of students were met with a bus pass and health card system. The Student Union now has a $1.5 million budget with twenty-one employees and administers seventy thousand square feet of space.

In 2005 Fanshawe College students made a $3 million commitment to the college's $15 million fundraising campaign with a pledge that will provide twenty percent of the goal.

The money will be raised with a $10 development charge levied on every student each semester until 2010.

Sports at the varsity and intramural level have always been

1980 BASKETBALL TEAM.

an important force in bringing Fanshawe students together.

Over the years Fanshawe Falcons have been a strong competitor in intervarsity sports. Fanshawe's initial Athletic Director, Les Zoltai, was a key player in the formation of the Ontario Colleges Athletic Association (OCAA) and later the Canadian Colleges Athletic Association (CCAA). Fanshawe teams now compete in men's and women's basketball, volleyball and soccer (outdoor and indoor) as well as badminton, cross-country running and golf. Over the years Fanshawe has also competed in curling, tennis, downhill skiing, table tennis, bowling and judo. The men's basketball team captured back-to-back CCAA national championships in 1979-80 and 1980-81. Fanshawe's Jim Matchett was national men's singles badminton champion in 1979 and the men's curling team were national champs in 1987-88. Fanshawe Falcon teams have also won about one hundred OCAA provincial championships over the years.

The Falcons men's hockey team was a major draw for fans playing games at the old London Gardens until the team had to be folded in 1982 due to budget restrictions.

Mike Lindsay, the current Athletics Director, graduated from the College's Recreation Leadership program in 1970 and went on to craft Fanshawe's popular intramural sports programs. Participation has always been the focus of the intramural program and thousands of students now play on the teams every year. Starting with five teams in 1970, the number of teams and sports has grown every year. The ball hockey league alone now has about sixty teams. "It's very much a tradition at Fanshawe to compete in intramurals for bragging rights and for camaraderie within the class," says Lindsay. Graduates returning for Homecoming inevitably reminisce about their intramural teams.

The Athletics program hit a new level in 1995 when a new $4.3 million double gym was constructed featuring a fifteen thousand square foot sprung wood floor. The new J building allowed Fanshawe to host national championships and athletic events. Fanshawe also partnered with the City of London to create a Community Fitness Centre allowing participation by sports groups and individuals across the city. The gym area underwent a $3.75 million expansion in 2002. The expansion replaced the old B-Gym and turned the facility into one of Ontario's top basketball and volleyball tournament sites.

Fanshawe in the Community

Over the years, Fanshawe has lived up to its mission as a "community" college. The College has graduated over 100,000 students and eighty-four percent of them have remained in the local community. One in six Londoners has attended Fanshawe as a full- or part-time student and it is difficult to find any major workplace in the London area that does not employ Fanshawe graduates. In London, Mayor Anne Marie DeCicco-Best, Police Chief Murray Faulkner and Fire Chief John Kobarda are all Fanshawe grads.

Other prominent former Fanshawe students include Oscar-winning filmmaker Paul Haggis, design guru Steven Sabodos, singer-songwriter Cassandra Vasik, singer-songwriter Emm Gryner, Dave Betts and Derry Grehan of the rock band Honeymoon Suite, Don Donner, Executive Director of the Boys' and Girls' Club of London, and charity fund-raiser Jesse Davidson.

The Fanshawe Alumni Association was founded in 1976 as a volunteer group. Bob Clark, the first Student Council President also served as the first Alumni Association President.

At that time the College had nine thousand graduates. In 1987, Mary Ann Darling, a Fanshawe graduate active in the Alumni Association, became Fanshawe's first Alumni Officer. The Association has helped bring Fanshawe grads in touch through its semi-annual publications and an annual Distinguished Alumni Awards program. The Association administers a number of awards, bursaries and athletic scholarships. Every year the Association reaches out to a class that graduated twenty-five years ago and organizes a reunion. The Alumni Association operates a Mentoring for Success program, which matches Fanshawe graduates with students studying in the same field.

Fanshawe also reaches into the community through its Continuing Education and job retraining programs. About forty thousand people attend Fanshawe courses annually to upgrade their skills in business management, computer software, marketing, customer service, accounting, health care and technical trades.

Fanshawe is also involved in international education projects in twelve countries including Ecuador, China, Indonesia, Egypt and Guyana.

Major corporations including Ellis-Don, John Deere, Nortel Networks, General Motors and Ford of Canada have partnered with Fanshawe in providing equipment and skills training to students.

As a leader in co-op programs, Fanshawe has formed a strong relationship with the business community in the London region. London Chamber of Commerce General Manager Gerry Macartney said the co-op programs give students valuable experience and serve as a great recruitment tool for employers. Recent community partnerships for Fanshawe's Business students include the development of search engine marketing strategies for local businesses, supported by Google. Students from the International Business Management program also help businesses take advantage of global marketing opportunities.

Fanshawe has also drawn on the generosity of the community through its fund-raising campaign. Fanshawe is capping its fortieth anniversary with the successful completion of a $15 million fund-raising campaign. Campaign chair Bob Siskind said the campaign has allowed for new and innovative programming, and new facilities such as an acute care paramedic lab and a manufacturing automation lab. Don and Joan Smith, who led Fanshawe's first fund-raising effort, agreed to serve as Honorary Co-Chairs for this campaign.

From its humble beginnings in 1967, Fanshawe College has become known as a "first choice" Canadian college – a place where students are the focus and alumni have become a strong, supportive force spread throughout the community. Harry Rawson, who was there from the beginning, said community colleges have developed their own identity after forty years. "Education was once seen as a ladder and you had to fit into one of the rungs. But these days it is more like a tree and colleges like Fanshawe are one of the branches."

"Discovery of Hands" sculpture in the B courtyard.

Acknowledgements

On my first tour of Fanshawe College, prior to starting the photography for this book, I was amazed at what I saw. Many times over the past 40 years, I had driven by this college, for the most part unaware of the complexity of the programs and facilities, which now makes this one of the finest community colleges in the country. The recent expansion and beatification, still underway, has dramatically changed the landscape along Oxford Street and Fanshawe College Boulevard. This is truly a gem in our academic crown.

So many people were instrumental in making this book happen. Thanks to President Howard Rundle, Emily Marcoccia and Cheryl McMurray for their unwavering vision, support and leadership. They have each given so much not only to this campus but also to making this book happen. I would also like to thank Hank Daniszewski for writing the historical section for this book. Hank and I worked together many years ago on a student newspaper, and his kindness and professionalism is still what makes him such a talented journalist.

It was an honour to have our London mayor and Fanshawe graduate, Anne Marie DeCicco-Best agree to write a personal foreword for the book. She is a great ambassador for this college and for our city, as evidenced so eloquently by her written reflections. She is yet another example of the high calibre of graduates that are making a significant difference in our community and around the world.

Thank you to all of the individuals who shared a reflective quote about Fanshawe. So many others, staff, faculty and students accommodated me in helping to capture the images from this remarkable place.

It is amazing how a designer can take a collection of images and text and produce a finished work. Amanda Jean Francis from Response Generators did just that, and I thank her for her patience in accommodating all of the changes that a photographer can throw her way. Thanks also to Tom Klassen from Friesens Book Division who was instrumental in the production.

I extend heartfelt thanks to my wife Joan, who always has time to look at my images at the end of a day. When you started Binea Press ten years ago, you likely had no idea that my photographic assignments would be this rewarding. I went back to school once more…this time at Fanshawe College, and learned so much. One of the last photographs I took for the book was of students working in a photo studio lab. As I left the studio, my hope was that they would derive as much enjoyment from this craft as I have.

I hope this book keeps the memory alive for those of you fortunate enough to have an affiliation with this great college. I am envious of those who have actually had the opportunity to spend more than the 10 months I did around this campus. May all who visit this campus once more, through these images and writings, remember how fortunate we all are for the gifts that Fanshawe College contributes to our community and the world.

Richard Bain